D1497833

EDITED BY HELEN EXLEY

Published in 2019 by Helen Exley®LONDON in Great Britain.
Illustration by Juliette Clarke © Helen Exley Creative Ltd 2019.
All the words by Amanda Bell, Odile Dormeuil, Pam Brown,
Charlotte Gray, Hannah C. Klein, Stuart & Linda Macfarlane,
Linda Gibson, Mathilde and Sébastian Forestier, Pamela Dugdale
© Helen Exley Creative Ltd 2019.
Design, selection and arrangement © Helen Exley Creative Ltd 2019.
The moral right of the author has been asserted.

ISBN 978-1-78485-202-3

12 11 10 9 8 7 6 5 4 3 2 1

OTHER BOOKS IN THE SERIES

THE LITTLE BOOK OF *Happiness*
THE LITTLE BOOK OF *Hope*
THE LITTLE BOOK OF *Kindness*
THE LITTLE BOOK OF *Smiles*

Helen Exley®LONDON
16 Chalk Hill, Watford, Herts WD19 4BG, UK
www.helenexley.com

THE LITTLE BOOK OF
Gratitude

Helen Exley

With every breath.
With every
heartbeat.
I give thanks
for simply
being alive.

BRIAN CLYDE

Every morning when I open
my curtains for that first look at the day,
no matter what the day looks like,
raining, foggy, overcast, sunny,
my heart swells with gratitude.
I get another chance.

OPRAH WINFREY

W hile you're waiting for
the big things delight in the little things
that come to hand.
And if by chance the big things never come,
you'll still have had a lovely life.

ODILE DORMEUIL

Each day provides

ts own gifts. MARTIAL

Make this a cappuccino day.
Make every moment sweet and exhilarating.

AMANDA BELL

Life is a neve

nding gift.

STUART & LINDA MACFARLANE

Gratitude unlocks the fullness of life.
It turns what we have into enough,
and more. It turns denial
into acceptance, chaos into order,
confusion to clarity.
It can turn a meal into a feast,
a house into a home,
a stranger into a friend.
Gratitude makes sense of our past,
brings peace for today,
and creates vision for tomorrow.

MELODY BEATTIE

When I wake in the morning
and discover that I'm still alive
I'm grateful — everything
that might happen during the day
is an added bonus.

BRIAN CLYDE

The person who has everything
and wants more has nothing.
The person who has nothing yet
is content has everything.

MATHILDE AND SÉBASTIEN FORESTIER

To love and be loved.
To like and to be liked.
To do work well.
To see and listen.
To learn.
That can fill a life to the brim.
That can be enough for anyone.

CHARLOTTE GRAY

Throw joy like

A fluke.

Another wiggle

and you would have never been.

Out of nothingness you came.

Out of star stuff.

Infinitely small changes

brought you to this.

To love.

To adventure.

To amazement.

PAM BROWN

onfetti. AUTHOR UNKNOWN

Think of what you have
rather than of what you lack.
Of the things you have,
select the best
and then reflect how eagerly
you would have sought them
if you did not have them.

MARCUS AURELIUS

Bread, water
and friendship.
And love
if we're lucky.
It's enough.

PAM BROWN

You see now what I live by –
the devotion and service of others.
I was blind, now I see;
I was deaf now I hear. I was dumb,
now I speak, and it was through
the hands of others that this miracle
was wrought in me.
It was through the hands of others
that I found myself,

found my mother and father,
found the world.
It is through the hands of others
that I, deaf and blind,
know the richness and fullness of life.
It is through the strength
of others that I am able
to do work that is worthwhile.

HELEN KELLER
(BORN BOTH DEAF AND BLIND)

Don't miss it!
Be grateful
for this moment —
you are in it!

BRIAN CLYDE

Each breath
is a blessing.
Each heartbeat
a joy.
Cherish each
special moment –
live life
with a smile.

LINDA GIBSON

You are surrounded
by gifts every
living moment
of every day.
Let yourself
feel appreciation
for their
presence
in your life
and take the time
to acknowledge
their splendor.

LON G. NUNGESSER

beautiful.

STUART & LINDA MACFARLANE

Gratitude can transform any situation.
It alters your vibration, moving you
from negative energy to positive.
It's the quickest, easiest, most powerful way
to effect change in your life
– this I know for sure.

OPRAH WINFREY

I have nothing to be thankful for...
Except the flowers that brighten up my life.
Except the rainbows
that fill my skies with joy.
Except the mountains and hills and rivers
that make my walks a delight.
Except the love, friendship
and companionship that make every one
of my days amazing!
I have nothing to be thankful for...
Except!

STUART & LINDA MACFARLANE

A kind word from a stranger
is a pearl that enriches your life.

LINDA GIBSON

The more we know the better we forgive.
Whoever feels deeply, feels for all who live.

MADAME DE STAEL

We can set our deeds to the music
of a grateful heart.

WILLIAM MACKERGO TAYLOR

They are wise
who do not grieve
for the things which
they don't have,
but rejoice for those
which they have.

EPICTETUS

Be thankful
for what you have,
you'll end up having more.
If you concentrate on
what you don't have,
you will never,
ever have enough.

OPRAH WINFREY

Gratitude is a debt which usually
goes on accumulating.

MARK TWAIN

To have been alive is a gift
beyond all others.
To have breathed air,
heard kind voices.
To have reached out towards a smile
and be engulfed in love.
To have known birdsong, sea surge,
skies awash with stars.
One flower, one leaf, one rainbow.
That is enough.
All else is richness beyond belief.

PAM BROWN

Friendship consists
in forgetting what one gives
and remembering
what one receives.

ALEXANDRE DUMAS

To the generous mind
the heaviest debt
is that of gratitude,
when it is not in our power
to repay it.

BENJAMIN FRANKLIN

I woke up this
morning with devout
thanksgiving
for my friends,
the old
and the new.

RALPH WALDO EMERSON

Fun.
Feel it.
Love it.
Live it.

LINDA MACFARLANE

H appiness does not come
boxed and labelled.
Cannot be supplied by manufacturers.
Grows wild.
Is all about you. Free.

HANNAH C. KLEIN

T he private and personal blessings
we enjoy, the blessings of immunity,
safeguard, liberty and integrity,
deserve the thanksgiving of a whole life.

JEREMY TAYLOR

Let us rise up and be thankful,
for if we didn't learn a lot today
at least we learned a little,
and if we didn't learn a little,
at least we didn't get sick,
and if we got sick,
at least we didn't die;
so let us all be thankful!

GAUTAMA BUDDHA

I don't look for perfection any more.
Right now is perfection.
I don't have to be the best
or the biggest any more.
The greatest joy is appreciation.
Once you have something in life
and almost lose it and manage
to get it back,
you learn about appreciation.

SID CAESAR

· ·∗· ·∗· ·∗·∗·∗··∗··

Be glad to

I desire to call your attention to the first
and plainest topics of gratitude.
They are close by. The best things
which they, who have them,
enjoy, are those which are common
to them with people of
the humblest condition.

RALPH WALDO EMERSON

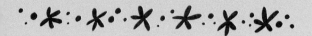

e alive.

PAM BROWN

Amidst the most unwelcome rain
there can often be found
a glorious rainbow.
Amidst life's pain
there are often amazing days
that shimmer an inspiration
to those who see.

MATHILDE AND SÉBASTIEN FORESTIER

Gratitude is the heart's memory.

FRENCH PROVERB

I live in the space of thankfulness
— and for that, I have been rewarded
a million times over.
I started out giving thanks for small things,
and the more thankful I became,
the more my bounty increased.
That's because – for sure –
what you focus on expands.

OPRAH WINFREY

Let us be grateful to people
who make us happy;
they are the charming gardeners
who make us blossom.

MARCEL PROUST

If I were any happi

'd be a Rainbow!

LINDA GIBSON

The essence of all beautiful art,
all great art, is gratitude.

FRIEDRICH WILHELM NIETZSCHE

Each day
is a gift,
each moment
a blessing.

STUART & LINDA MACFARLANE

If the future is filled with days
like today I will be completely satisfied.

LINDA GIBSON

Gratitude is not only
the greatest of virtues, but the parent
of all the others.

MARCUS TULLIUS CICERO

There is not a day goes by
that I don't discover something new
and wonderful to be grateful for.

BRIAN CLYDE

In the morning, how good it is
to see the brilliant light
of the blessed summer day,
always brightest just after rain,
and to see how every tree and plant
is full of new life and abounding gladness;
and to feel one's own thankfulness
of heart, and that it is good to live...

GERTRUDE JEKYLL

Some people are
always grumbling
because roses
have thorns;
I am thankful
that thorns
have roses.

ALPHONSE KARR

Everyone has been gifted with
a unique talent; some may be
world class gymnasts, others may
have an angelic singing voice.
There are those whose talents may appear
less obvious. Their talent may be
the ability to be an empathetic,
understanding friend or an ability
to find ways to raise money for charity.
These talents are very important;
they should be nurtured
and very much cherished.

STUART MACFARLANE

Never forget that the essence of
abundance is not just material wealth.
Having a grateful heart
and an appreciation for life itself –
for what we have made of our lives,
as well as what we have been given –
is the most blessed of all forms
of abundance.

CHRISTIANE NORTHRUP

I love the first and last
The whole field of the present view,
The whole flow of the past.
One tittle of the things that are.
Nor should you change nor I
One pebble in our path – one star
In all our heaven of sky.

ROBERT LOUIS STEVENSON

Be happy
in your times of joy
Be brave
in your times of pain
Be courageous
in your times of sorrow
Be grateful
for all the times of your life.

STUART & LINDA MACFARLANE

Running in the park.
The sky when it's dark.
A nice glass of wine.
Friends round to dine.
They all fill my days with wonder.
New-born lambs.
Babies in their prams.
Flowers smelling sweet.
Chocolate to eat.
They all fill my days.

STUART MACFARLANE

The softest, comforting sigh,
a hug, a gentle word –
all vital!
All appreciated! All precious!

MATHILDE AND SÉBASTIEN FORESTIER

Gratitude is the inward feeling
of kindness received.
Thankfulness is the natural impulse
to express that feeling.
Thanksgiving is the following
of that impulse.

HENRY VAN DYKE

Be grateful
for this
moment.
It is yours.

STUART & LINDA MACFARLANE

A child's hand rests in yours.
A bird sings.
A dragon-fly gleams above the lake.
A star falls.
Any sorrow is a little price to pay
for this great wonder.

PAMELA DUGDALE

Be grateful for everything
that you have for you have more
than you could ever need.

BRIAN CLYDE

The power of finding
beauty in the
humblest things
makes home happy
and life lovely.

LOUISA MAY ALCOTT

I thank the flowers.
I thank the grass
for being green,
I thank the sky for
being so high.

AMANDA BELL

Gratefulness is the key to a happy life
that we hold in our hands, because if we
are not grateful, then no matter
how much we have we will not be happy –
because we will always want to have
something else or something more.

DAVID STEINDL-RAST

The more you praise and celebrate your life, the more there is in life to celebrate.

OPRAH WINFREY

Praise the bridge tha

arried you over.

GEORGE COLMAN – THE YOUNGER

Only a few have genius.

And it's a hard thing to wear.

The rest of us must play out

more ordinary parts

– each of us necessary,

vital to the whole.

Taking the gifts that others won for us,

using them as wisely as we can,

with gratitude.

ODILE DORMEUIL

Whatever hour god has blessed you with,
take it with grateful hand,
nor postpone your joys from year to year,
so that, in whatever place you have been,
you may say that you have lived happily.

HORACE

To be alive is something set
against fantastic odds.
Each of us is an astonishment.
Treasure each moment
that was denied to countless millions.

CHARLOTTE GRAY

The still
small voice
of gratitude.

THOMAS GRAY

Take any
happiness
with
grateful
hands.

ODILE DORMEUIL

We should always consider
how much we have more
than we want, and how much
more unhappy we might be
than we really are.

JOSEPH ADDISON

Life is a joyous gift to be enjoyed
from the first breath
to the last, in grateful pleasure.

LINDA GIBSON

Live life
like a child
with an
ice-cream,
gleefully
whizzing down
the helter-skelter
of happiness
without a care
in the world.

STUART & LINDA MACFARLANE

Gratitude is when memory is stored
in the heart and not in the mind.

SAM N. HAMPTON

It's a funny thing about life,
once you begin to take note
of the things you are grateful for,
you begin to lose sight
of the things that you lack.

GERMANY KENT

Learn appreciation.
Be willing to take lovingly
each small gift of life
and receive it and acknowledge
that you have received it,
and appreciate it
and allow it in.
You won't be happy
with more until you're happy
with what you've got.

VIKI KING

To have lived long enough to see the sun,
the dapple of leaves, star-studded skies
and kindly faces –
to have heard the wind, birdsong,
loving voices,
to have touched a little cat,
a woollen blanket, a flower,
to have tasted clear water, fresh bread, honey,
to have breathed the perfume of a rose
– is enough to make any life worth the living.

PAM BROWN

There is beauty around us, in things large and
small, in friends, family, the countryside,
a singing bird. Stop to reflect, to give thanks,
to contemplate the gift of another day.
Touch the wonders of life and rejoice.

ANTON CHEKHOV

With my first sight of the spring crocus
my heart smiled in gratitude
for another year well lived.

LINDA MACFARLANE

Each step in Winter snow,
Each sparkle of Spring sunlight,
Each crunch of Autumn leaves,
Each sparkle of Summer sunlight,
Spell - REJOICE IN NOW!

STUART & LINDA MACFARLANE

And did you get what you wanted
from this life, even so?
I did. And what did you want? To call myself
beloved, to feel myself beloved on the earth.

RAYMOND CARVER

One of the greatest
treasures in the world
is a contented heart.

JOHN O'DONOHUE

I would maintain that thanks
are the highest form of thought; and that
gratitude is happiness doubled by wonder.

G. K. CHESTERTON

Life is a gift to be opened slowly
and cherished.

MATHILDE AND SÉBASTIEN FORESTIER

I am building my future brick by brick.
Yesterday I had a Bunkhouse
of contentment, today a Bungalow
of satisfaction, tomorrow,
success by success,
I will have a castle of happiness
and delight.

STUART MACFARLANE

As we express our gratitude, we must never forget that the highest appreciation is not to utter words, but to live by them.

PRESIDENT JOHN F. KENNEDY

Happiness is spilling from my cup. My life is overflowing.

STUART & LINDA MACFARLANE

Happiness does not lead us
to be thankful – rather thankfulness
will lead us to be happy.

AMANDA BELL

At the close of each day take a moment
just to recall all the positive
and precious thoughts and experiences
that brought you joy!

BRIAN CLYDE

What you focus on expands,
and when you focus on the goodness
in your life, you create more of it.
Opportunities, relationships, even money
flowed my way when I learned to be grateful
no matter what happened in my life.

OPRAH WINFREY

Life is so rare a gift
that any price is worth the paying.
To have lived is to have been given
treasures beyond belief.
– Treasures that can never
be taken from us.
Stars and daisies, oceans and rain.
Love and kindness.

MARK DUGDALE

I think the thing is
always to look ahead in life,
and never look back,
except in gratitude
for happy times past.

DAPHNE DU MAURIER

I don't think then of all the misery,
but of the beauty that still remains.
My advice is: "Go outside,
to the fields, enjoy nature
and the sunshine, go out
and try to recapture happiness.
Think of all the beauty that's still left in
and around you and be happy!"

ANNE FRANK

Every day I endeavour
to do three things before breakfast...
Have a positive thought.
Smile at the wonder of nature.
Say thank you for a kindness.

MATHILDE AND SÉBASTIEN FORESTIER

In our daily lives, we must see
that it is not happiness
that makes us grateful, but the gratefulness
that makes us happy.

ALBERT CLARKE

There can be few better ways
to spend a morning
than walking in the countryside.
To have your senses filled
with nature's wide wonders –
of rabbits and deer,
of rivers and lakes
and sweet scented wild rose
and heather.
And all around the sound
of cuckoos and skylarks.

STUART & LINDA MACFARLANE

There is not
a minute in
the twenty-four
hours that is
not filled
with miracles...

RALPH WALDO EMERSON

The World
belongs to those
who have
nothing,
yet are happy.

LINDA GIBSON

My thanks for this wonderful day.
I am grateful for
an abundance of happiness.

STUART & LINDA MACFARLANE

I find great happiness
in simple pleasures.

AMANDA BELL

With every beat your heart
is celebrating the miracle of life.

MATHILDE AND SÉBASTIEN FORESTIER

I don't have to have millions
of dollars to be happy.
All I need is to have some
clothes on my back,
eat a decent meal when I want to,
and get a little loving when I feel like it.
That's the bottom line, man.

RAY CHARLES

I am thankful for this day. I will take it
gratefully and fashion it in the image of
Friendship, Love and Happiness.

BRIAN CLYDE

No land belongs unto me,
Yet I can go out in the meadows and see
The healthy green grass –
and behold the shower fall,
And he that feels this,
who can say he is poor?

JOHN CLARE

Thankfulness transforms the world.

Turns acquaintances into friends.

Makes mediocre days feel good.

Helps dry tears of sorrow.

Opens eyes to the wonders of nature.

When we appreciate our blessings

everything becomes

much more pleasurable.

STUART & LINDA MACFARLANE

I thought
I was alone;
then someone
sent me
flowers.

CHRISTINA ANELLO

Life is a miracle.
You are a miracle.
Love the miracle.

STUART & LINDA MACFARLANE

I murmured because
I had no shoes,
until I met someone
who had no feet.

PERSIAN PROVERB

If you haven't all the things
that you want in this world,
just be grateful for the things you don't have
that you never wanted.

CHINESE PROVERB

At times our own light
goes out and is rekindled by a spark
from another person.
Each of us has cause to think
with deep gratitude of those
who have lighted the flame within us.

ALBERT SCHWEITZER

Not to understand a treasure's worth,
Till time has stolen away the slightest good,
Is cause of half the poverty we feel,
And makes the world the wilderness it is.

WILLIAM COWPER

It is not so much our friends'
help that helps us as
the confident knowledge
that they will help us.

EPICURUS

${A}$ hundred times a day I remind myself
that my inner and outer life
depends on the labours of other people,
living and dead, and that I must
exert myself to give in the same measure
as I have received.

ALBERT EINSTEIN

We have thousands of opportunities every day to be grateful: for having good weather, to be able to sit in such a beautiful room on such comfortable furniture, to have slept well last night, to be able to get up, to be healthy, to have enough to eat. There's opportunity upon opportunity to be grateful; that's what life is.

DAVID STEINDL-RAST

${W}$henever you can't think of something to be grateful for, remember your breath. With each breath you take, you can say, "I am still here." Make each day a holiday of thankfulness – and give yourself the gift of gratitude.

OPRAH WINFREY

${B}$e at peace with yourself, be at peace with the world. All is well. All will continue to be well.

MATHILDE AND SÉBASTIEN FORESTIER

${I}$ can no other answer make but thanks. And thanks, and ever thanks.

WILLIAM SHAKESPEARE